COOKING WITH OLIVE OIL

SIMPLY DELICIOUS OLIVE OIL COOKING WITH OVER 50 OLIVE OIL RECIPES

By
BookSumo Press
Copyright © by Saxonberg Associates
All rights reserved

Published by
BookSumo Press, a DBA of Saxonberg Associates
http://www.booksumo.com/

ABOUT THE AUTHOR.

BookSumo Press is a publisher of unique, easy, and healthy cookbooks.

Our cookbooks span all topics and all subjects. If you want a deep dive into the possibilities of cooking with any type of ingredient. Then BookSumo Press is your go to place for robust yet simple and delicious cookbooks and recipes. Whether you are looking for great tasting pressure cooker recipes or authentic ethic and cultural food. BookSumo Press has a delicious and easy cookbook for you.

With simple ingredients, and even simpler step-by-step instructions BookSumo cookbooks get everyone in the kitchen chefing delicious meals.

BookSumo is an independent publisher of books operating in the beautiful Garden State (NJ) and our team of chefs and kitchen experts are here to teach, eat, and be merry!

INTRODUCTION

Welcome to *The Effortless Chef Series*! Thank you for taking the time to purchase this cookbook.

Come take a journey into the delights of easy cooking. The point of this cookbook and all BookSumo Press cookbooks is to exemplify the effortless nature of cooking simply.

In this book we focus on methods of cooking with olive oil. You will find that even though the recipes are simple, the taste of the dishes are quite amazing.

So will you take an adventure in simple cooking? If the answer is yes please consult the table of contents to find the dishes you are most interested in.

Once you are ready, jump right in and start cooking.

— BookSumo Press

TABLE OF CONTENTS

About the Author 2

Introduction 3

Table of Contents 4

Any Issues? Contact Us 10

Legal Notes 11

Common Abbreviations 12

Chapter 1: Easy Olive Oil Recipes 13

    Asparagus Couscous Salad 13

    Simply Roasted Rosemary Mushrooms 15

    Beginner's Parmesan Risotto I 17

    Parmesan and Penne 20

    Elegant Primavera 22

Buttery Shrimp with Egg Noodles 25

Asparagus Penne 27

Angel Hair and Mushrooms... 29

Portobello Stuffed Pasta 31

Asparagus Casserole 33

Low Carb Asparagus Appetizer... 36

Buttery Capers and Tilapia 38

Perfect Scallops.. 40

Eggplant, Basil, Feta Sandwich.. 43

Balsamic Mushroom Sandwich... 45

Pepperoncini Sandwich 48

Maggie's Favorite Italian Style Sandwich 50

SoCal Sandwich 52

(Vegetarian Approved) 52

The Athenian Dream Sandwich 55

Tandoori Apple Asiago Sandwich 58

Soy Sandwich... 60

(Vegetarian Approved) 60

Lemon and Bacon Stuffed Chicken 63

Lamb & Potato Pot Pie 65

Mushroom and Beef Pot Pie 68

Orzo, Leeks, and Sherry Soup 71

Savory Fritters 73

Artisan Chicken and Squash 76

Mayan Couscous 79

Catalina's Mexican Rice 81

Quinoa Tacos 83

(Vegan Approved) 83

Grilled Herbed Veggies 85

Pesto Spinach and Tomatoes 87

Roasted Cauliflower, Garlic, and Leek Soup 89

Shawarma 92

Cheesy Spaghetti 95

Soup of Carrots and Lentils 98

Dolmas 100

(Stuffed Grape Leaves) 100

Greek Style Shrimp 103

Classical Hummus I 105

Greek Style Salad Dressing 107

Pasta from Athens 109

Greek Style Macaroni Salad 111

Pita, Pesto, and Parmesan 113

(Greek Style Bake) 113

Greek Spinach Puff Pastry Bake 115

Greek Spinach Puff Pastry Bake 118

Souvlaki III 121

Easy Greek Style Chicken Breasts 124

Baked Greek Potatoes 127

Greek Rice 129

Parsley Pasta Salad 131

Orzo Salad II 133

Mediterranean Dijon Shrimp Salad 135

Easy Greek Penne and Steak 138

Rustic Potatoes with Oregano and Olives 141

Shrimp with Feta and Tomatoes 143

Classical Mediterranean Salad Dressing 146

Mediterrean Asian Salad Dressing 148

Homemade Balsamic Salad Dressing 150

Sesame Blueberry Salad Dressing 152

Latin Omelet 154

Coconut Chicken Breast 156

Ensalada Roja con Pollo 159

(Latin Potato Salad) 159

Broccoli Bake I 162

(Red Onions and Sage) 162

Italian Style Broccoli and Pasta 164

Easy Broccoli Stir Fry 166

THANKS FOR READING! JOIN THE CLUB AND KEEP ON COOKING WITH 6 MORE COOKBOOKS... 168

Come On... 170

Let's Be Friends :).. 170

Any Issues? Contact Us

If you find that something important to you is missing from this book please contact us at info@booksumo.com.

We will take your concerns into consideration when the 2nd edition of this book is published. And we will keep you updated!

— BookSumo Press

Legal Notes

ALL RIGHTS RESERVED. NO PART OF THIS BOOK MAY BE REPRODUCED OR TRANSMITTED IN ANY FORM OR BY ANY MEANS. PHOTOCOPYING, POSTING ONLINE, AND / OR DIGITAL COPYING IS STRICTLY PROHIBITED UNLESS WRITTEN PERMISSION IS GRANTED BY THE BOOK'S PUBLISHING COMPANY. LIMITED USE OF THE BOOK'S TEXT IS PERMITTED FOR USE IN REVIEWS WRITTEN FOR THE PUBLIC.

COMMON ABBREVIATIONS

cup(s)	C.
tablespoon	tbsp
teaspoon	tsp
ounce	oz.
pound	lb

*All units used are standard American measurements

Chapter 1: Easy Olive Oil Recipes

Asparagus Couscous Salad

Ingredients

- 2 C. couscous
- 1 bunch fresh asparagus, trimmed and cut into 2-inch pieces
- 8 oz. grape tomatoes, halved
- 6 oz. feta cheese, crumbled
- 3 tbsps balsamic vinegar
- 2 tbsps extra-virgin olive oil
- Black pepper, to taste

Directions

- Prepare your couscous in-line with the directions on its box before doing anything else. Then let it cool.
- Simultaneously, with a steamer insert, and 2 inches of boiling water, steam your asparagus for 7 mins with a lid on the pot.
- Get a big bowl, mix: olive oil, couscous, pepper, asparagus, vinegar, feta, and tomatoes.
- Enjoy.

Amount per serving (4 total)

Timing Information:

Preparation	10 m
Cooking	20 m
Total Time	30 m

Nutritional Information:

Calories	541 kcal
Fat	16.7 g
Carbohydrates	77.7g
Protein	20.1 g
Cholesterol	38 mg
Sodium	494 mg

* Percent Daily Values are based on a 2,000 calorie diet.

Simply Roasted Rosemary Mushrooms

Ingredients

- 1 bunch fresh asparagus, trimmed
- 1/2 lb. fresh mushrooms, quartered
- 2 sprigs fresh rosemary, minced
- 2 tsps olive oil
- kosher salt to taste
- freshly ground black pepper to taste

Directions

- Coat a baking sheet with nonstick spray and then set your oven to 450 degrees before doing anything else.
- Get a bowl, toss: pepper, asparagus, salt, mushrooms, rosemary, and olive oil.
- Evenly distribute the veggies throughout the sheet and cook them in the oven for 17 mins.
- Enjoy.

Amount per serving (6 total)

Timing Information:

Preparation	10 m
Cooking	15 m
Total Time	25 m

Nutritional Information:

Calories	38 kcal
Fat	1.8 g
Carbohydrates	4.3g
Protein	2.8 g
Cholesterol	0 mg
Sodium	84 mg

* Percent Daily Values are based on a 2,000 calorie diet.

Beginner's Parmesan Risotto I

Ingredients

- 20 fresh asparagus spears, trimmed
- 4 C. low-sodium chicken broth
- 2 tbsps olive oil
- 1 small onion, diced
- 1 stalk celery, diced
- 1/4 tsp salt
- 1/4 tsp ground black pepper1 clove garlic, minced
- 1 C. arborio rice
- 1/2 C. dry white wine
- 1/4 C. freshly grated Parmesan cheese
- 2 tbsps lemon juice
- 1/2 tsp lemon zest

Directions

- With a steamer insert, steam your asparagus for 7 mins, with 2 inches of water.
- Now slice the spears into bite sized pieces.
- Get your broth boiling in a large pot and then lower the heat for a light simmer.

- Get a frying pan and stir fry your celery and onions for 6 mins in olive oil and then add in the rice and garlic and continue cooking for 6 more mins.
- Now add in the wine and cook for 6 more mins.
- Create a risotto by adding 1 ladle of simmering broth to the rice.
- Let it absorb into the rice and then add another ladle full.
- While adding the broth stir the contents. Once you have added the broth let everything cook for 20 mins then pour in your asparagus.
- Shut the heat and add your lemon juice, parmesan, and zest.
- Enjoy.

Amount per serving (4 total)

Timing Information:

Preparation	15 m
Cooking	45 m
Total Time	1 h

Nutritional Information:

Calories	357 kcal
Fat	8.7 g
Carbohydrates	53.4g
Protein	11.1 g
Cholesterol	8 mg
Sodium	355 mg

* Percent Daily Values are based on a 2,000 calorie diet.

Parmesan and Penne

Ingredients

- 1 (16 oz.) package dried penne pasta
- 5 tbsps olive oil, divided
- 2 skinless, boneless chicken breast halves - cut into cubes
- salt and pepper to taste
- garlic powder to taste1/2 C. low-sodium chicken broth
- 1 bunch slender asparagus spears, trimmed, cut on diagonal into 1-inch pieces
- 1 clove garlic, thinly sliced
- 1/4 C. Parmesan cheese

Directions

- Boil your pasta in salt and water for 9 mins. The remove all the liquid.
- Coat your chicken with garlic powder, pepper, and salt before frying them in olive oil (3 tbsps) for 7 mins. Place everything on paper towels to remove excess oils.
- Add the broth to the pan and then add: pepper, asparagus, salt, garlic, and garlic powder.
- Cook the asparagus with a lid on the pan for 8 mins. Then add in your chicken and heat it up again.
- Add the pasta to the pan and let everything rest for 7 mins. Add in parmesan and 2 tbsps of olive oil before serving.
- Enjoy.

Amount per serving (8 total)

Timing Information:

Preparation	15 m
Cooking	20 m
Total Time	35 m

Nutritional Information:

Calories	332 kcal
Fat	10.9 g
Carbohydrates	43.3g
Protein	16.7 g
Cholesterol	20 mg
Sodium	69 mg

* Percent Daily Values are based on a 2,000 calorie diet.

Elegant Primavera

Ingredients

- 1 (12 oz.) package penne pasta
- 1 yellow squash, chopped
- 1 zucchini, chopped
- 1 carrot, cut into matchsticks
- 1/2 red bell peppers, cut into matchsticks
- 1/2 pint grape tomatoes
- 1 C. fresh green beans, trimmed and cut into 1 inch pieces
- 5 spears asparagus, trimmed and cut into 1 inch pieces
- 1/4 C. olive oil, divided
- 1 tbsp Italian seasoning
- 1/2 tbsp lemon juice
- 1/4 tsp salt
- 1/4 tsp coarsely ground black pepper
- 1 tbsp butter
- 1/4 large yellow onion, thinly sliced
- 2 cloves garlic, thinly sliced
- 2 tsps lemon zest
- 1/3 C. chopped fresh basil leaves
- 1/3 C. chopped fresh parsley
- 3 tbsps balsamic vinegar
- 1/2 C. grated Romano cheese

Directions

- Layer foil inside a casserole dish and then set your oven to 450 degrees before doing anything else.
- Cook your pasta in salt and water for 11 mins.

- Get a bowl, toss: asparagus, salt, Italian seasoning, pepper, squash, beans, olive oil (2 tbsp), zucchini, tomatoes, lemon juice, carrots, and bell pepper.
- Evenly distribute the veggies throughout the casserole dish.
- Cook everything in the oven for 17 mins.
- Stir fry your garlic and onions in butter and olive oil for 6 mins.
- Then add in: vinegar, pasta, parsley, lemon zest, and basil.
- Cook the mix for 6 more mins. Then place everything in a bowl.
- Add in the veggies after they have finished cooking and then garnish everything with your Romano.
- Enjoy.

Amount per serving (6 total)

Timing Information:

Preparation	25 m
Cooking	35 m
Total Time	1 h

Nutritional Information:

Calories	406 kcal
Fat	15.4 g
Carbohydrates	54.4g
Protein	13.6 g
Cholesterol	15 mg
Sodium	252 mg

* Percent Daily Values are based on a 2,000 calorie diet.

BUTTERY SHRIMP WITH EGG NOODLES

Ingredients

- 1 lb. fresh asparagus
- 1 (16 oz.) package egg noodles
- 4 cloves garlic, minced
- 1/2 C. extra virgin olive oil
- 1 C. butter
- 1 tbsp lemon juice
- 1 lb. medium shrimp - peeled and deveined
- 1 lb. fresh mushrooms, thinly sliced
- 1/2 C. grated Parmesan cheese
- salt and pepper to taste

Directions

- With a steamer insert, steam your asparagus for 5 mins until tender but firm, over 2 inches of water.
- Then cut the spears into bite sized pieces.
- Stir fry your garlic until golden in olive oil. Then add in lemon juice and butter.
- Once the butter is melted add in the shrimp and cook them until pink.
- Now throw in your asparagus and mushrooms and keep stir frying the mix until the mushrooms are soft.
- Add your egg noodles to the veggies and top them with parmesan.
- Now toss everything and add your preferred amount of pepper and salt before tossing again.
- Enjoy.

Amount per serving (8 total)

Timing Information:

Preparation	20 m
Cooking	30 m
Total Time	50 m

Nutritional Information:

Calories	653 kcal
Fat	42.2 g
Carbohydrates	45.4g
Protein	24.7 g
Cholesterol	199 mg
Sodium	340 mg

* Percent Daily Values are based on a 2,000 calorie diet.

Asparagus Penne

Ingredients

- 1 (16 oz.) package dry penne pasta
- 2 tbsps olive oil, divided
- 3/4 lb. skinless, boneless chicken breast meat - cut into bite-size pieces
- 4 cloves garlic, minced
- 12 oz. asparagus, trimmed and cut into 1 inch pieces
- 1 tsp crushed red pepper flakes
- salt and pepper to taste
- 1/2 C. grated Parmesan cheese

Directions

- Cook your pasta in boiling water with salt for 9 mins.
- Then remove the liquid and place the pasta in a bowl.
- Stir fry your chicken in 1 tbsp of olive oil. Then take the chicken out and place it to the side. Add in the rest of the olive oil to the pan and stir fry your asparagus and garlic for 6 mins then add the pepper flakes.
- Once the asparagus is soft add the chicken and cook for 3 more mins add pepper and salt and then the pasta.
- Stir fry the contents to evenly distribute the meat and then top with parmesan.
- Enjoy.

Amount per serving (8 total)

Timing Information:

Preparation	15 m
Cooking	20 m
Total Time	35 m

Nutritional Information:

Calories	311 kcal
Fat	6.8 g
Carbohydrates	43.2g
Protein	20.3 g
Cholesterol	29 mg
Sodium	113 mg

* Percent Daily Values are based on a 2,000 calorie diet

Angel Hair and Mushrooms

Ingredients

- 1 1/2 lb. fresh asparagus, trimmed and cut into 1 inch pieces
- 1/4 C. chicken broth
- 1/2 lb. fresh mushrooms, sliced
- 8 oz. angel hair pasta
- 1 tbsp olive oil
- 1/2 tsp crushed red pepper
- 1/2 C. grated Parmesan cheese

Directions

- Boil your pasta in water and salt for 7 to 9 mins then remove all the liquid.
- Stir fry your asparagus in olive oil for 4 mins then add the broth and mushrooms cook the contents for 5 more mins.
- Now pour in the pasta with the asparagus and stir to coat.
- When serving the dish top it with parmesan.
- Enjoy.

Amount per serving (4 total)

Timing Information:

Preparation	15 m
Cooking	10 m
Total Time	25 m

Nutritional Information:

Calories	281 kcal
Fat	8.4 g
Carbohydrates	39.4g
Protein	15.5 g
Cholesterol	9 mg
Sodium	339 mg

* Percent Daily Values are based on a 2,000 calorie diet.

Portobello Stuffed Pasta

Ingredients

- 1 tbsp butter
- 1 tbsp olive oil
- 1 lb. portobello mushrooms, stems removed, cut in half to 1/4 of an inch in thickness
- 1/2 tsp salt
- 1 1/4 C. low-sodium chicken broth
- 1 (5.2 oz.) package pepper Boursin cheese
- 3/4 lb. uncooked pasta shells
- 1 lb. fresh asparagus, trimmed

Directions

- Boil your pasta in water and salt for 7 mins then add the asparagus and continue cooking for 5 more mins. Now remove all the liquid.
- Stir fry the mushrooms in olive oil and butter for 9 mins. Then add in your salt.
- Add the cheese and the broth and get the contents lightly simmering.
- Continue stirring until everything is blended evenly.
- Pour the sauce over the asparagus and toss to coat the pasta evenly.
- Enjoy

Amount per serving (6 total)

Timing Information:

Preparation	15 m
Cooking	25 m
Total Time	40 m

Nutritional Information:

Calories	400 kcal
Fat	16.6 g
Carbohydrates	51.6g
Protein	14.1 g
Cholesterol	35 mg
Sodium	388 mg

* Percent Daily Values are based on a 2,000 calorie diet.

Asparagus Casserole

Ingredients

- 1 (8 oz.) package egg noodles
- 1 1/3 tbsps olive oil
- 1 onion, chopped
- 1 C. chopped, cooked chicken meat
- 1 red bell pepper, chopped
- 2 stalks celery, chopped
- 1 C. chicken stock
- 1 1/2 C. sour cream
- 1/2 tsp dried oregano
- 1 lb. fresh asparagus, trimmed and cut into 2 inch pieces
- 8 tbsps grated Parmesan cheese, divided

Directions

- Coat a baking dish with nonstick spray and then set your oven to 350 degrees before doing anything else.
- Boil your pasta in water and salt for 7 mins then remove all the liquid.
- Stir fry your onions for 6 mins in olive oil then combine in: chicken stock, chicken, celery, and bell peppers.
- Get everything boiling, lower the heat, and let the contents simmer for 5 mins.
- Add in the oregano and sour cream.
- Layer half of the chicken mix in the casserole dish and then top the mix with asparagus, pasta, and 5 tbsps of parmesan.
- Add the rest of the chicken and add the rest of the parmesan as well.
- Cook the casserole in the oven for 30 mins.

- Enjoy.

Amount per serving (6 total)

Timing Information:

Preparation	30 m
Cooking	45 m
Total Time	1 h 15 m

Nutritional Information:

Calories	376 kcal
Fat	20.1 g
Carbohydrates	32.7g
Protein	17.3 g
Cholesterol	77 mg
Sodium	323 mg

* Percent Daily Values are based on a 2,000 calorie diet.

Low Carb Asparagus Appetizer

Ingredients

- 1 tbsp olive oil
- 16 spears fresh asparagus, trimmed
- 16 slices prosciutto

Directions

- Cover the insides of a casserole dish with foil and then coat the foil with olive oil.
- Now set your oven to 450 degrees before doing anything else.
- Wrap your asparagus in prosciutto and evenly distribute them through the casserole dish.
- Continue for all the spears.
- Cook everything in the oven for 7 mins and then turn the spears and cook for 5 more mins.
- Enjoy hot.

Amount per serving (16 total)

Timing Information:

Preparation	5 m
Cooking	15 m
Total Time	20 m

Nutritional Information:

Calories	64 kcal
Fat	5.4 g
Carbohydrates	0.6g
Protein	< 3.1 g
Cholesterol	13 mg
Sodium	279 mg

* Percent Daily Values are based on a 2,000 calorie diet.

Buttery Capers and Tilapia

Ingredients

- 2 (3 oz.) fillets tilapia fillets
- 2 tbsps olive oil
- salt and pepper to taste
- 1 lemon, halved
- 1/2 C. white wine
- 2 tomatoes, seeded and chopped
- 3 tbsps capers
- 1 C. asparagus spears, trimmed and cut in half
- 3 tbsps butter

Directions

- Top your fish with olive oil, half of the lemon, pepper and salt. Cook for 4 min per side in a pan with medium heat. Set everything to the side.
- Now add to the pan: pepper, wine, salt, the rest of lemon, capers, and tomatoes.
- Boil everything for 3 mins and then add in the asparagus and the fish sauce.
- Lower the heat and place a lid on the pan. Now cook the mix for 3 mins. Finally place everything in a dish.
- Add some more butter to the same pan and heat the butter for 3 mins until it begins to boil.
- Top your fish with the butter.
- Enjoy.

Amount per serving (2 total)

Timing Information:

Preparation	15 m
Cooking	15 m
Total Time	30 m

Nutritional Information:

Calories	462 kcal
Fat	32.6 g
Carbohydrates	16.3g
Protein	21.4 g
Cholesterol	77 mg
Sodium	1726 mg

* Percent Daily Values are based on a 2,000 calorie diet.

Perfect Scallops

Ingredients

- 1 (16 oz.) package medium seashell pasta
- 6 tbsps butter
- 1 tbsp olive oil
- 1 tbsp chopped fresh parsley
- 1 clove garlic, chopped
- 1 (10 oz.) package sliced fresh button mushrooms
- 1 bunch asparagus, trimmed and cut into 1 inch pieces
- salt and pepper to taste
- 1/2 tsp onion powder
- 1 lb. scallops, rinsed and patted dry
- 1/4 C. milk
- 1 (8 oz.) container mascarpone cheese
- 2 tbsps butter

Directions

- Boil your pasta in water and salt for 8 mins. Then remove the liquid.
- Now fry your garlic and parsley in butter (6 tbsps) until aromatic.
- Then add: asparagus, mushrooms, onion powder, salt, and pepper.
- Stir fry this mix for 6 mins.
- Now add the scallops and cook them for 4 mins each side.
- In a separate pan mix the following: butter, milk, and cheese.
- Stir and cook this mix until everything is smooth.
- Pour the butter sauce over the scallops and asparagus.

- Now pour in your pasta and toss to coat everything.
- Enjoy hot.

Amount per serving (6 total)

Timing Information:

Preparation	15 m
Cooking	20 m
Total Time	35 m

Nutritional Information:

Calories	714 kcal
Fat	37.8 g
Carbohydrates	63.2g
Protein	35.3 g
Cholesterol	134 mg
Sodium	360 mg

* Percent Daily Values are based on a 2,000 calorie diet.

Eggplant, Basil, Feta Sandwich

Ingredients

- 1 small eggplant, halved and sliced
- 1 tbsp olive oil, or as needed
- 1/4 C. mayonnaise
- 2 cloves garlic, minced
- 2 (6 inch) French sandwich rolls
- 1 small tomato, sliced
- 1/2 C. crumbled feta cheese
- 1/4 C. minced fresh basil leaves

Directions

- Turn on your broiler to low if possible.
- Get a bowl, mix: garlic and mayo.
- Take your eggplant pieces and coat them with olive oil. Put them on a sheet for baking.
- For 10 mins cook the eggplant in the broiler 6 inches from the heat.
- Cut your French bread in half and toast it.
- Spread a good amount of mayo and garlic mix on your bread and layer the following to form a sandwich: tomato, basil leaves, eggplant, and feta.
- Enjoy.

Amount per serving (2 total)

Timing Information:

Preparation	Cooking	Total Time
20 m	10 m	30 m

Nutritional Information:

Calories	802 kcal
Fat	39.5 g
Carbohydrates	91.3g
Protein	23.8 g
Cholesterol	44 mg
Sodium	1460 mg

* Percent Daily Values are based on a 2,000 calorie diet.

Balsamic Mushroom Sandwich

Ingredients

- 2 cloves garlic, minced
- 6 tbsps olive oil
- 1/2 tsp dried thyme
- 2 tbsps balsamic vinegar
- salt and pepper to taste
- 4 large Portobello mushroom caps
- 4 hamburger buns
- 1 tbsp capers
- 1/4 C. mayonnaise
- 1 tbsp capers, drained
- 1 large tomato, sliced
- 4 leaves lettuce

Directions

- Preheat your broiler and set its rack so that it is near the heating source before doing anything else.
- Get a bowl and mix: pepper, garlic, salt, olive oil, vinegar, and thyme.
- Get a 2nd bowl, combine: mayo and capers.
- Coat your mushrooms with half of the dressing.
- Then toast the veggies for 5 mins under the broiler.
- Flip the mushrooms after coating the opposite side with the remaining dressing.
- Toast everything for 5 more mins.
- Now also toast your bread.

- Apply some mayo to the bread before layering a mushroom, some lettuce and tomato.
- Enjoy.

Amount per serving (4 total)

Timing Information:

Preparation	Cooking	Total Time
8 m	9 m	20 m

Nutritional Information:

Calories	445 kcal
Fat	33.4 g
Carbohydrates	31.4g
Protein	7.8 g
Cholesterol	5 mg
Sodium	426 mg

* Percent Daily Values are based on a 2,000 calorie diet.

Pepperoncini Sandwich

Ingredients

- 2 thick slices whole wheat bread
- 2 tbsps cream cheese, softened
- 6 slices cucumber
- 2 tbsps alfalfa sprouts
- 1 tsp olive oil
- 1 tsp red wine vinegar
- 1 tomato, sliced
- 1 leaf lettuce
- 1 oz. pepperoncini, sliced
- 1/2 avocado, mashed

Directions

- Layer one piece of bread with the following: 1 tbsp of cream cheese, alfalfa sprouts, oil and vinegar, cucumber pieces, tomatoes, pepperoncini, and lettuce.
- Coat another piece of bread with avocado and form a sandwich.
- Enjoy.

Amount per serving (1 total)

Timing Information:

Preparation	Cooking	Total Time
10 m		10 m

Nutritional Information:

Calories	496 kcal
Fat	32.5 g
Carbohydrates	46.3g
Protein	11.4 g
Cholesterol	32 mg
Sodium	1024 mg

* Percent Daily Values are based on a 2,000 calorie diet.

Maggie's Favorite Italian Style Sandwich

Ingredients

- 1 (1 lb) loaf fresh Italian bread
- 1/3 C. olive oil
- 1/3 C. grated Parmesan cheese
- 1 tbsp dried basil
- 1 tbsp dried oregano
- 8 oil-cured black olives, pitted and minced
- 8 pitted green olives, minced
- 1/4 lb thinly sliced salami
- 1/4 lb thinly sliced turkey ham
- 1/2 lb provolone cheese, sliced
- 1/4 lb mozzarella cheese, sliced

Directions

- Cut your bread in half then coat one side with: olive oil, oregano, parmesan, and basil.
- Add the following to the other piece: green olives, mozzarella, black olives, provolone, ham and salami.
- Form everything into a sandwich and divide it into multiple pieces.
- Enjoy.

Amount per serving (4 total)

Timing Information:

Preparation	Cooking	Total Time
15 m		15 m

Nutritional Information:

Calories	975 kcal
Fat	59.9 g
Carbohydrates	61.3g
Protein	46.2 g
Cholesterol	107 mg
Sodium	2790 mg

* Percent Daily Values are based on a 2,000 calorie diet.

SoCal Sandwich

(Vegetarian Approved)

Ingredients

- 1/4 C. mayonnaise
- 3 cloves garlic, minced
- 1 tbsp lemon juice
- 1/8 C. olive oil
- 1 C. sliced red bell peppers
- 1 small zucchini, sliced
- 1 red onion, sliced
- 1 small yellow squash, sliced
- 2 (4-x6-inch) focaccia bread pieces, split horizontally
- 1/2 C. crumbled feta cheese

Directions

- Get a bowl, combine: lemon juice, mayo, and minced garlic.
- Place a covering of plastic on the bowl and put everything in the fridge.
- Now get your outdoor grill hot and coat the grate with oil.
- Lay your zucchini and bell peppers in the center of the grate then spread the squash and onions around the peppers.
- Grill the veggies for 5 mins then flip them and continue grilling for 4 more mins.
- Now remove everything from the grill.

- Coat your pieces of bread with the mayo mix liberally then add some feta to each.
- Lay your bread on the grill with the cheese facing upwards and toast the bottoms of the bread for 4 mins.
- Top the sandwiches evenly with the veggies and serve open faced.
- Enjoy.

Amount per serving (4 total)

Timing Information:

Preparation	Cooking	Total Time
30 m	20 m	50 m

Nutritional Information:

Calories	393 kcal
Fat	23.8 g
Carbohydrates	36.5g
Protein	9.2 g
Cholesterol	22 mg
Sodium	623 mg

* Percent Daily Values are based on a 2,000 calorie diet.

Cooking with Olive Oil

The Athenian Dream Sandwich

Ingredients

- 4 Italian-style hoagie buns, split lengthwise
- 1/4 C. chopped fresh basil

Artichoke Aioli:

- 1 (6.5 oz.) jar marinated artichoke hearts, drained
- 2 tbsps mayonnaise
- 2 tbsps grated Parmesan cheese
- 1 tsp lemon zest
- 1/2 lemon, juiced
- 1/4 tsp red pepper flakes
- salt and ground black pepper to taste

Filling:

- 2 tbsps olive oil
-
- 1 1/2 lbs beef tri-tip steak, thinly sliced
- 1 tsp Italian seasoning
- 1 onion, sliced thin
- 1 yellow bell pepper, sliced into strips
- 1 orange bell pepper, sliced into strips
- 1/4 C. pickled sweet and hot pepper rings
- 1/4 C. garlic basil spread (see footnote for recipe link)
- 1 C. sliced mushrooms
- 1 tbsp capers
- 1 tbsp Marsala wine
- 1 anchovy fillet (optional)
- 12 slices aged provolone cheese
- 1/4 C. crumbled Gorgonzola cheese

Directions

- Puree the following with a food processor: black pepper, artichoke, salt, mayo, pepper flakes, parmesan, lemon juice, and lemon zest.
- Add the mix to a bowl and place a covering of plastic over the bowl.
- Put everything in the fridge.
- Begin to stir fry your steak, in a saucepan, in olive oil, for 5 mins then top the meat with some black pepper, salt, and the Italian spice.
- Stir the spice into the meat then combine in: garlic basil spread, onions, sweet hot pepper, yellow pepper, and orange pepper.
- Stir the mix and cook everything for 7 mins then combine in: the anchovy, mushrooms, Marsala, and capers.
- Let the mix cook for 6 more mins.
- Add in your cheese and let it melt (2 to 4 more mins of heating).
- Now shut the heat.
- Liberally coat your rolls with the parmesan artichoke sauce, then with a liberal amount of steak mix.
- Top everything with basil and serve.
- Enjoy.

Amount per serving (8 total)

Timing Information:

Preparation	Cooking	Total Time
30 m	15 m	45 m

Nutritional Information:

Calories	681 kcal
Fat	36.4 g
Carbohydrates	44.9g
Protein	43.7 g
Cholesterol	108 mg
Sodium	1087 mg

* Percent Daily Values are based on a 2,000 calorie diet.

Tandoori Apple Asiago Sandwich

Ingredients

- 1 apple, cored and chopped
- 1/3 bunch kale, chopped
- 1 tbsp tandoori seasoning
- 1 tsp cayenne pepper
- 1/4 C. apple cider
- 1 tbsp olive oil
- 4 slices bacon
- 3 large cracked wheat dinner-style rolls, split
- 3 tbsps grated Asiago cheese

Directions

- Fry your bacon for 11 mins then place the bacon on some paper towel to drain.
- Begin to stir the following in the apple cider, apples, cayenne, kale, and tandoori spice.
- Top the mix with the olive oil as it fries in the bacon fat and let everything cook for 8 mins. Then place the mix to the side.
- Evenly coat the bottom piece of the bread with the tandoori mix then with some bacon and asiago.
- Form sandwiches with the other half of the bread.
- Enjoy.

Amount per serving (3 total)

Timing Information:

Preparation	Cooking	Total Time
15 m	15 m	30 m

Nutritional Information:

Calories	342 kcal
Fat	21.9 g
Carbohydrates	30.5g
Protein	9.5 g
Cholesterol	26 mg
Sodium	492 mg

* Percent Daily Values are based on a 2,000 calorie diet.

Cooking with Olive Oil

Soy Sandwich

(Vegetarian Approved)

Ingredients

- 1 (12 oz.) package firm tofu - drained, patted dry, and sliced into 4 slices
- 1 C. bread crumbs
- 1 tsp kelp powder
- 1/4 tsp garlic powder
- 1/4 tsp paprika
- 1/4 tsp onion powder or flakes
- 1 tsp salt
- olive oil, as needed
- Tartar Sauce
- 1/2 C. mayonnaise
- 1/4 C. dill pickle relish
- 1 tbsp fresh lemon juice
- 4 whole wheat hamburger buns, split

Directions

- Set your oven to 350 degrees before doing anything else.
- Get a bowl, combine: salt, bread crumbs, onion powder, kelp powder, paprika, and garlic powder.
- Coat your pieces of tofu with some olive oil then dredge them in the dry mix.
- Lay the tofu in a jellyroll pan and cook them in the oven for 35 mins.
- Watch the tofu and flip the pieces once the top side is browned.
- At the same time get a bowl and combine: lemon juice, mayo, and relish.

- Stir the mix until it is smooth.
- When about 5 mins of baking time is left. Coat the tofu with some olive oil and continue cooking everything.
- When eating your tofu dip the pieces in the relish mix.
- Enjoy.

Amount per serving (4 total)

Timing Information:

Preparation	Cooking	Total Time
15 m	30 m	45 m

Nutritional Information:

Calories	622 kcal
Fat	41.6 g
Carbohydrates	43.7g
Protein	21.4 g
Cholesterol	11 mg
Sodium	1332 mg

* Percent Daily Values are based on a 2,000 calorie diet.

Cooking with Olive Oil

Lemon and Bacon Stuffed Chicken

Ingredients

- 8 tbsps olive oil
- 2 tsps lemon juice
- 4 cloves crushed garlic
- 1 tbsp dried oregano
- salt and pepper to taste
- 4 skinless, boneless chicken breasts
- 4 slices feta cheese
- 4 slices bacon, fried and drained

Directions

- Set your oven to 350 degrees before doing anything else.
- Get a bowl, mix: pepper, oils, salt, lemon juice, and garlic.
- Fill your chicken pieces with 1 piece of bacon and 1 piece of feta. Then stake a toothpick through each.
- Layer your chicken in a casserole dish and coat them with the wet oil mix. Cook everything in the oven for 33 mins.
- Enjoy.

Amount per serving (4 total)

Timing Information:

Preparation	15 m
Cooking	30 m
Total Time	45 m

Nutritional Information:

Calories	483 kcal
Fat	37.1 g
Carbohydrates	3.2g
Protein	33.8 g
Cholesterol	100 mg
Sodium	529 mg

* Percent Daily Values are based on a 2,000 calorie diet.

Lamb & Potato Pot Pie

Ingredients

- 1 tbsp olive oil
- 1 tbsp butter
- 1 onion, diced
- 2 lbs lean ground lamb
- 1/3 C. all-purpose flour
- salt and ground black pepper to taste
- 2 tsps minced fresh rosemary
- 1 tsp paprika
- 1/8 tsp ground cinnamon
- 1 tbsp ketchup
- 3 cloves garlic, minced
- 2 1/2 C. water, or as needed
- 1 (12 oz.) package frozen peas and carrots, thawed
- 2 1/2 lbs Yukon Gold potatoes, peeled and halved
- 1 tbsp butter
- 1 pinch ground cayenne pepper
- 1/4 C. cream cheese
- 1/4 lb Irish cheese, shredded
- salt and ground black pepper to taste
- 1 egg yolk
- 2 tbsps milk

Directions

- Set your oven to 375 degrees before doing anything else.
- Stir fry your onions and lamb in butter and olive oil for 12 mins in a Dutch oven. Then break up the lamb.
- Then add the following to your lamb: garlic, flour, ketchup, salt, cinnamon, pepper, paprika, and rosemary. Cook for 4 more mins.

- Add in your water and get everything boiling. Once boiling, lower the heat so everything is only lightly boiling and then let the contents go for 7 mins.
- Shut off the heat and add your carrots and peas.
- Pour everything into a casserole dish.
- Boil the potatoes in salt and water for 17 mins.
- Remove all the liquid.
- Now mash your potatoes with: Irish cheese, butter, cream cheese, and cayenne. Finally add your preferred amount of pepper and salt.
- Get a bowl, mix: milk and egg yolks.
- Then combine with the potatoes.
- Enter the potatoes with the lamb in the casserole dish.
- Cook everything in the oven for 35 mins.
- Enjoy after letting the dish sit for 5 mins.

Amount per serving (10 total)

Timing Information:

Preparation	Cooking	Total Time
25 m	1 h 10 m	1 h 35 m

Nutritional Information:

Calories	413 kcal
Fat	22.6 g
Carbohydrates	29.8g
Protein	23.3 g
Cholesterol	106 mg
Sodium	210 mg

* Percent Daily Values are based on a 2,000 calorie diet.

Mushroom and Beef Pot Pie

Ingredients

- 3 tbsps olive oil, divided
- 1 lb cubed beef stew meat
- 2 slices bacon, diced
- 1 white onion, diced
- 1 carrot, sliced
- 1/3 lb crimini mushrooms, sliced
- 1 clove garlic, crushed
- 1 tsp white sugar
- 1 1/2 tbsps all-purpose flour
- 1 C. Irish beer
- 1 1/4 C. beef stock
- 1/2 tsp ground thyme
- 2 bay leaves
- 1/2 tsp cornstarch, or as needed
- 1 tsp water
- 1 sheet frozen puff pastry, thawed
- 1 egg, beaten

Directions

- Fry your beef in 2 tbsps of olive oil for 12 mins. Then place everything to the side.
- Fry your bacon in 1 tbsp of olive oil for a few mins and then add in sugar, onions, garlic, mushrooms, and carrots. Stir fry everything for 16 mins until tender.
- Add in your flour and mix evenly. Then slowly add in the stock and beer.
- Once the stock and beer has been incorporated. Add the bay leaves, and thyme.

- Get everything boiling then place a lid on the pan and lower the heat.
- Let the contents lightly boil for 1 hr and 20 mins.
- Then take off the lid and let everything keep boiling for 20 more mins to thicken the sauce.
- Add your cornstarch and water and let everything simmer for 32 mins.
- After 15 mins of simmering set your oven to 350 degrees before doing anything else.
- Line a pie dish with puff pastry and fill the pie with the stew.
- Cover the stew with more puff pastry.
- Seal the edges with a utensil (large fork) and then cut some openings into the pie. Top with whisked eggs. Cook in the oven for 40 mins.
- Enjoy.

Amount per serving (6 total)

Timing Information:

Preparation	Cooking	Total Time
25 m	2 h 35 m	3 h

Nutritional Information:

Calories	500 kcal
Fat	31.7 g
Carbohydrates	28.6g
Protein	21.8 g
Cholesterol	77 mg
Sodium	259 mg

* Percent Daily Values are based on a 2,000 calorie diet.

ORZO, LEEKS, AND SHERRY SOUP

Ingredients

- 4 oz. fresh mushrooms, sliced
- 1 C. sliced leeks
- 2 tbsps margarine
- 2 tbsps olive oil
- 1/2 C. dry sherry
- 3 (10.5 oz.) cans condensed beef broth
- 3 3/4 C. water
- 1/2 tsp ground black pepper
- 1/2 C. uncooked orzo pasta

Directions

- Fry your leeks and mushrooms in olive oil until they are soft. Then pour in your sherry and simmer the liquid until half of it evaporates.
- Combine your pepper, broth, and water. Get everything boiling. Once boiling, mix in your orzo.
- Let the contents boil for 13 mins.
- When serving the soup top with freshly sliced or diced mushrooms.
- Enjoy.

Amount per serving (6 total)

Timing Information:

Preparation	Cooking	Total Time
15 m	35 m	50 m

Nutritional Information:

Calories	182 kcal
Fat	8.4 g
Carbohydrates	19.6g
Protein	6.7 g
Cholesterol	6 mg
Sodium	1233 mg

* Percent Daily Values are based on a 2,000 calorie diet.

Savory Fritters

Ingredients

- 1 head cauliflower, broken into small florets
- 1 onion
- 7 sprigs fresh parsley
- 5 cloves garlic, crushed
- 1 1/2 C. all-purpose flour
- 1 tsp salt
- 1/4 tsp ground black pepper
- 1 tsp ground cumin
- 1 tsp ground allspice
- 1/2 tsp ground cinnamon
- 1/4 tsp ground cloves
- 1/4 tsp ground nutmeg
- 1 tsp active dry yeast
- 1 C. warm water
- 1/4 C. vegetable oil
- 1/4 C. olive oil
- 4 eggs

Directions

- Boil your cauliflower for 12 mins then remove the liquids from the pot and let the veggies sit.
- Add your parsley and onions to the bowl of a food processor and mince them with a few pulses.
- Now drain the mix.
- Get a bowl, combine: nutmeg, flour, cloves, salt, cinnamon, pepper, allspice, and cumin.
- Stir the mix then top everything with the dry yeast.

- Stir the mix again then add in the crushed garlic and the warm water.
- Combine everything then place a covering of plastic on the bowl and let the contents sit for 12 mins.
- Now get your veggie and olive oil hot to 365 degrees before doing anything else.
- Whisk your eggs then combine them with the parsley, onions, and cauliflower.
- Stir the mix then combine everything with the dough.
- Now add a bit of flour of the mix if it is too wet or add some more water if it is too thick.
- Once the batter is the right consistency begin to fry large dollops of the mix in the oil.
- Fry everything, 4 at a time, until golden.
- Enjoy.

Amount per serving (12 total)

Timing Information:

Preparation	30 m
Cooking	30 m
Total Time	1 h

Nutritional Information:

Calories	184 kcal
Fat	11.3 g
Carbohydrates	16.4g
Protein	5.3 g
Cholesterol	62 mg
Sodium	326 mg

* Percent Daily Values are based on a 2,000 calorie diet.

Artisan Chicken and Squash

Ingredients

- 1 (3 lb) spaghetti squash
- 2 tbsps olive oil
- 1 onion, thinly sliced
- 2 cloves garlic, minced
- 1 green bell pepper, diced
- 2 tbsps paprika
- 1 tsp salt
- 1 tsp caraway seeds
- ground black pepper to taste
- 3 skinless, boneless chicken breast halves
- 1 (14.5 oz.) can whole peeled tomatoes, drained
- 1/2 C. sour cream (optional)

Directions

- Set your oven to 350 degrees before doing anything else.
- Bake your squash for 45 mins after punching some holes into it with a fork.
- After 45 mins rotate the squash and cook for 8 more mins.
- Now remove it from the oven.
- Once the squash has cooled off cut it in half, and discard the seeds.
- Scrape out the flesh with a fork and place the squash meat to the side.
- Stir fry your: black pepper, onions, caraway, garlic, salt, bell peppers, and paprika in olive oil for 7 mins then place everything to the side as well.
- Now cook your chicken until fully done for 11 mins per side.
- Take out the chicken from the pan and cut it in half diagonally.

- Place the chicken back into the pan with the onions and tomatoes. Once it is all simmering add in your scraped squash.
- Let the contents simmer for 12 mins. Then add in some sour cream before serving.
- Enjoy.

Amount per serving (6 total)

Timing Information:

Preparation	Cooking	Total Time
30 m	1 h 30 m	2 h

Nutritional Information:

Calories	251 kcal
Fat	11.5 g
Carbohydrates	25.5g
Protein	15.1 g
Cholesterol	39 mg
Sodium	561 mg

* Percent Daily Values are based on a 2,000 calorie diet.

Mayan Couscous

Ingredients:

- 1 cup couscous
- 1/2 tsp ground cumin
- 1 tsp salt, or to taste
- 1 1/4 cups boiling water
- 1 clove unpeeled garlic
- 1 (15 oz.) can black beans, rinsed and drained
- 1 cup canned whole kernel corn, drained
- 1/2 cup finely chopped red onion
- 1/4 cup chopped fresh cilantro
- 1 jalapeno pepper, minced
- 3 tbsps olive oil
- 3 tbsps fresh lime juice, or to taste

Directions:

- Add boiling water into a mixture of salt and couscous in a large sized bowl, and cover it with plastic wrap before letting it stand for about ten minutes.
- In this time, cook unpeeled garlic in hot oil over medium heat until it has turned golden brown.
- Now mash this garlic and add it into the couscous along with black beans, onion, cilantro, corn, jalapeno pepper, olive oil, and lime juice.
- Serve.

Serving: 15

Timing Information:

Preparation	Cooking	Total Time
15 min		25 min

Nutritional Information:

Calories	300 kcal
Carbohydrates	44.8 g
Cholesterol	0 mg
Fat	10.9 g
Fiber	3.6 g
Protein	7.1 g
Sodium	713 mg

* Percent Daily Values are based on a 2,000 calorie diet.

Catalina's Mexican Rice

Ingredients:

- 2 tbsps olive oil
- 1 cup rice
- 1/2 large onion, diced
- 1/2 tbsp salt
- 1/8 tsp ground cumin
- 1/8 tsp ground black pepper
- 2 1/2 cups water
- 1/3 cup tomato sauce
- 1 tbsp chicken bouillon
- 1 whole serrano chili pepper (optional)

Directions:

- Cook onion and rice in hot oil at medium heat for about 5 minutes or until golden brown and add pepper, salt and cumin.
- Now pour in some water over this mixture before adding chicken bouillon and tomato sauce.
- Bring this to a boil over medium heat after covering.
- Now add some chili pepper and cook for another 10 minutes.
- Now turn the heat down to low and cook for another 20 minutes.
- Let cool. Serve and enjoy.

Serving: 6

Timing Information:

Preparation	Cooking	Total Time
10 min	30 min	40 min

Nutritional Information:

Calories	164 kcal
Carbohydrates	26.8 g
Cholesterol	1 mg
Fat	4.9 g
Fiber	0.9 g
Protein	2.7 g
Sodium	845 mg

* Percent Daily Values are based on a 2,000 calorie diet.

Quinoa Tacos
(Vegan Approved)

Ingredients:

- 1 tsp olive oil
- 1 onion, chopped
- 2 (8 oz.) cans tomato sauce
- 1 1/2 cups water
- 1/2 cup quinoa
- 1 (1 oz.) envelope taco seasoning mix
- 2 (14.5 oz.) cans black beans, rinsed and drained
- 24 corn tortillas

Directions:

- Cook onion in hot oil for about 10 minutes before adding tomato sauce, taco seasoning, water and quinoa, and bring this mixture to a boil.
- Turn the heat down and cook for 15 minutes before adding black beans and cooking for another 5 minutes.
- Fill tortillas with this mixture and serve.

Serving: 8

Timing Information:

Preparation	Cooking	Total Time
15 min	25 min	40 min

Nutritional Information:

Calories	339 kcal
Carbohydrates	65.4 g
Cholesterol	0 mg
Fat	3.9 g
Fiber	13.8 g
Protein	13 g
Sodium	985 mg

* Percent Daily Values are based on a 2,000 calorie diet.

Grilled Herbed Veggies

Ingredients

- 2 tbsps olive oil
- 2 tbsps chopped fresh parsley
- 2 tbsps chopped fresh oregano
- 2 tbsps chopped fresh basil
- 1 tbsp balsamic vinegar
- 1 tsp kosher salt
- 1/2 tsp black pepper
- 6 cloves garlic, minced
- 1 red onion, cut into wedges
- 18 spears fresh asparagus, trimmed
- 12 crimini mushrooms, stems removed
- 1 (1 lb) eggplant, sliced into 1/4 inch rounds
- 1 red bell pepper, cut into wedges
- 1 yellow bell pepper, cut into wedges

Directions

- In a large resealable bag, add oil, vinegar, fresh herbs, garlic, salt and pepper and shake to mix.
- Add the vegetables and tightly, seal the bag and refrigerate to marinate for about 2 hours, flipping occasionally.
- Set your grill to high heat and grease the grill grate.
- Cook the vegetables on the grill for about 12 minutes, flipping once half way.

Amount per serving (6 total)

Timing Information:

Preparation	15 m
Cooking	12 m
Total Time	2 h 30 m

Nutritional Information:

Calories	107 kcal
Fat	4.9 g
Carbohydrates	13.3g
Protein	4.3 g
Cholesterol	0 mg
Sodium	340 mg

* Percent Daily Values are based on a 2,000 calorie diet.

Pesto Spinach and Tomatoes

Ingredients

- 2 tbsps olive oil
- 2 garlic cloves, coarsely chopped
- 1 bunch fresh spinach, chopped
- 1 pint cherry tomatoes, halved
- 2 tbsps prepared basil pesto

Directions

- In a large skillet, heat oil on medium heat and sauté garlic for about 1 minute.
- Add spinach and stir fry for about 2 minutes or till wilted.
- Stir in tomatoes and cook for about 2 minutes.
- Stir in the pesto and serve hot.

Amount per serving (2 total)

Timing Information:

Preparation	10 m
Cooking	5 m
Total Time	15 m

Nutritional Information:

Calories	272 kcal
Fat	21.8 g
Carbohydrates	15.1g
Protein	9.1 g
Cholesterol	5 mg
Sodium	267 mg

* Percent Daily Values are based on a 2,000 calorie diet.

Roasted Cauliflower, Garlic, and Leek Soup

Ingredients

- 1 head cauliflower, cut into florets
- 3 tbsps olive oil
- salt and ground black pepper to taste
- 4 cloves garlic
- 1/4 C. butter
- 2 stalks celery
- 1 leek - split, cleaned, and minced
- 1/4 C. all-purpose flour
- 4 C. chicken broth
- 1 tsp dried marjoram

Directions

- Set your oven to 400 degrees F before doing anything else and grease a baking sheet.
- In a bowl, add cauliflower and drizzle with oil and sprinkle with salt and black pepper.
- Spread the cauliflower and garlic into the prepared baking sheet and Cook everything in the oven for about 15 minutes.
- Flip the cauliflower and garlic and sauté for about 10 minutes.
- In a large pan, melt butter on medium heat and sauté the leeks and celery for about 5 minutes or till softened.

- Stir in the flour and cook, stirring continuously for about 2-3 minutes.
- Add the broth, stirring continuously till well combined.
- Stir in the cauliflower mixture and marjoram and bring to a gentle simmer and cook for about 10 minutes.
- Remove everything from the heat and with an immersion blender, puree the soup to the desired consistency.
- Season with salt and black pepper and serve hot.

Amount per serving (4 total)

Timing Information:

Preparation	15 m
Cooking	45 m
Total Time	1 h

Nutritional Information:

Calories	292 kcal
Fat	22.5 g
Carbohydrates	19.4g
Protein	5.5 g
Cholesterol	36 mg
Sodium	1145 mg

* Percent Daily Values are based on a 2,000 calorie diet.

Shawarma

Ingredients

- 1 tbsp ground coriander
- 1 tbsp ground cumin
- 1 tbsp ground cardamom
- 1 tbsp chili powder
- 1 tbsp grill seasoning
- 1 tsp smoked paprika
- 1/2 tsp ground turmeric
- 1 lemon, juiced, divided
- 1 large clove garlic, minced
- 5 tbsps extra-virgin olive oil, divided
- 4 (6 oz.) skinless, boneless chicken breast halves
- 1 large onion, sliced
- 1 red bell pepper, sliced
- 1 yellow bell pepper, sliced
- salt and ground black pepper to taste
- 1 1/2 C. Greek yogurt
- 1/4 C. tahini
- 1 tsp extra-virgin olive oil
- 4 pita bread rounds

Directions

- Set your outdoor grill to high heat and grease the grill grate.
- In a large bowl, add spices, garlic, 1/2 of lemon juice and 3 tbsps of oil and mix till a paste forms.
- Add the chicken breasts and coat with paste generously.
- Cook on the grill for about 12 minutes, flipping once half way or till desired doneness.

- Place the chicken breasts onto a plate and let them cool and then cut into thin slices.
- In a large skillet, heat 2 tbsps of oil on medium heat and sauté the bell peppers and onion with salt and black pepper for about 5 minutes.
- In a bowl, mix together yogurt, tahini, remaining lemon juice, 1 tsp of oil and salt.
- Cook the pita on grill for about 1 minute per side or till lightly charred.
- Divide chicken and bell pepper mixture over pita breads evenly.
- Serve with a topping of tahini yogurt.

Amount per serving (4 total)

Timing Information:

Preparation	20 m
Cooking	20 m
Total Time	45 m

Nutritional Information:

Calories	737 kcal
Fat	39.6 g
Carbohydrates	46.4g
Protein	49.1 g
Cholesterol	114 mg
Sodium	1133 mg

* Percent Daily Values are based on a 2,000 calorie diet.

Cheesy Spaghetti

Ingredients

- 1 lb spaghetti
- 1 tbsp olive oil
- 8 slices bacon, diced
- 1 tbsp olive oil
- 1 onion, chopped
- 1 clove garlic, minced
- 1/4 C. dry white wine
- 4 eggs
- 1/2 C. grated Parmesan cheese
- pinch of salt and black pepper
- 2 tbsps chopped fresh parsley
- 2 tbsps grated Parmesan cheese

Directions

- In a large pan of lightly salted boiling water, add the spaghetti and cook the spaghetti till desired doneness and drain well.
- In a bowl, add the spaghetti and 1 tbsp of the oil and toss to coat well and keep aside.
- Meanwhile heat a large skillet and cook the bacon till crisp.
- Transfer the bacon onto a paper towel lined plate, leaving 2 tbsps of fat in the skillet.
- In the same skillet, heat the remaining 1 tbsp of the oil with bacon fat on medium heat and sauté the onion till tender.
- Stir in the garlic and sauté for about 1 minute.
- Stir in the wine and cook for 1 minute further.

- Stir in the cooked spaghetti and bacon and toss till heated completely.
- Stir in the eggs and cook, tossing continuously till the eggs set.
- Stir in 1/2 C. of the cheese till well combined.
- Stir in the salt and black pepper and remove from heat.
- Serve immediately with a garnishing of the remaining cheese and parsley.

Amount per serving (8 total)

Timing Information:

Preparation	20 m
Cooking	20 m
Total Time	40 m

Nutritional Information:

Calories	444 kcal
Fat	21.1 g
Carbohydrates	44.7g
Protein	16.4 g
Cholesterol	118 mg
Sodium	369 mg

* Percent Daily Values are based on a 2,000 calorie diet.

Soup of Carrots and Lentils

Ingredients

- 8 oz. brown lentils
- 1/4 C. olive oil
- 1 tbsp minced garlic
- 1 onion, minced
- 1 large carrot, chopped
- 1 quart water
- 1 pinch dried oregano
- 1 pinch crushed dried rosemary
- 2 bay leaves
- 1 tbsp tomato paste
- salt and ground black pepper to taste
- 1 tsp olive oil, or to taste
- 1 tsp red wine vinegar, or to taste (optional)

Directions

- Submerge your lentils, in water, in a big pot, and get it all boiling.
- Once it is boiling let the contents cook for 12 mins then remove all the liquids.
- Stir fry the carrots, onions, and garlic in olive oil for 7 mins then add in: bay leaves, lentils, rosemary, water (1 qt.), and oregano.
- Get everything boiling again, place a lid on the pot, and let the contents gently cook over a low level of heat for 12 mins.
- Now add in some pepper, salt, and your tomato paste.
- Place the lid back on the pot and cook everything for 35 more mins.
- Finally add in some olive oil and red wine vinegar before serving.
- Enjoy.

Amount per serving (4 total)

Timing Information:

Preparation	20 m
Cooking	1 h
Total Time	1 h 20 m

Nutritional Information:

Calories	357 kcal
Fat	15.5 g
Carbohydrates	40.3g
Protein	15.5 g
Cholesterol	0 mg
Sodium	57 mg

* Percent Daily Values are based on a 2,000 calorie diet.

Dolmas

(Stuffed Grape Leaves)

Ingredients

- 2 C. uncooked long-grain white rice
- 1 large onion, chopped
- 1/2 C. chopped fresh dill
- 1/2 C. chopped fresh mint leaves
- 2 quarts chicken broth
- 3/4 C. fresh lemon juice, divided
- 60 grape leaves, drained and rinsed
- hot water as needed
- 1 C. olive oil

Directions

- Stir fry the following for 7 mins: onions, rice, and dill.
- Now add in half of the broth and cook the mix for 17 mins with low level heat and a gentle boil.
- Add in half of the lemon juice and shut the heat.
- Layer 1 tsp of rice mix into the center of one grape leaf.
- Now roll this leaf into the shape of a burrito.
- Continue for all of your rice mix and then place all of the rolls into a big pot.
- Top everything in the pot with olive oil, broth, and lemon juice.

- Now place a lid on the pot and cook the mix for 65 mins with a low level of heat.
- You want to avoid boiling this mix.
- Shut the heat and let the rolls sit for 40 mins before layering them in a casserole dish to serve.
- Enjoy.

Amount per serving (12 total)

Timing Information:

Preparation	40 m
Cooking	1 h
Total Time	1 h 40 m

Nutritional Information:

Calories	303 kcal
Fat	18.7 g
Carbohydrates	30.9g
Protein	3.6 g
Cholesterol	0 mg
Sodium	573 mg

* Percent Daily Values are based on a 2,000 calorie diet.

Greek Style Shrimp

Ingredients

- 1 lb. medium shrimp, with shells
- 1 onion, chopped
- 2 tbsps chopped fresh parsley
- 1 C. white wine
- 1 (14.5 oz.) can diced tomatoes, drained
- 1/4 tsp garlic powder (optional)
- 1/4 C. olive oil
- 1 (8 oz.) package feta cheese, cubed
- salt and pepper to taste (optional)

Directions

- Submerge your shrimp in water and boil them for 7 mins, then drain all the liquids and place the shrimp in a bowl.
- Stir fry your onions in 2 tbsps of olive oil until tender and then add: the rest of the olive oil, parsley, garlic powder, wine, and tomatoes.
- Cook this mix with a low heat and a gentle boil for 35 mins.
- At the same time remove the skins of the shrimp but leave the head and tails intact.
- After 35 mins of cooking the tomatoes, add in the shrimp, and cook for 7 more mins.
- Combine in the feta and shut the heat. Let the contents sit for 10 mins.
- Enjoy.

Amount per serving (4 total)

Timing Information:

Preparation	5 m
Cooking	35 m
Total Time	40 m

Nutritional Information:

Calories	441 kcal
Fat	26.6 g
Carbohydrates	10.1g
Protein	27.8 g
Cholesterol	223 mg
Sodium	1093 mg

* Percent Daily Values are based on a 2,000 calorie diet.

Classical Hummus I

Ingredients

- 2 C. canned garbanzo beans, drained
- 1/3 C. tahini
- 1/4 C. lemon juice
- 1 tsp salt
- 2 cloves garlic, halved
- 1 tbsp olive oil
- 1 pinch paprika
- 1 tsp minced fresh parsley

Directions

- Blend the following in a food processer until paste-like: garlic, garbanzos, salt, tahini, and lemon juice.
- Add this to a bowl with olive oil, paprika, and parsley.
- Enjoy.

Amount per serving (16 total)

Timing Information:

Preparation	
Cooking	10 m
Total Time	10 m

Nutritional Information:

Calories	77 kcal
Fat	4.3 g
Carbohydrates	8.1g
Protein	2.6 g
Cholesterol	0 mg
Sodium	236 mg

* Percent Daily Values are based on a 2,000 calorie diet.

Greek Style Salad Dressing

Ingredients

- 1 1/2 quarts olive oil
- 1/3 C. garlic powder
- 1/3 C. dried oregano
- 1/3 C. dried basil
- 1/4 C. pepper
- 1/4 C. salt
- 1/4 C. onion powder
- 1/4 C. Dijon-style mustard
- 2 quarts red wine vinegar

Directions

- Get bowl, combine: Dijon, olive oil, onion powder, garlic powder, salt, oregano, pepper, and basil.
- Now add in the vinegar and mix everything nicely.
- Place a covering over the bowl and serve the contents once all the ingredients have reached room temp.
- Enjoy the dish over romaine lettuce and diced sun dried tomatoes.

Amount per serving (120 total)

Timing Information:

Preparation	
Cooking	10 m
Total Time	10 m

Nutritional Information:

Calories	104 kcal
Fat	10.8 g
Carbohydrates	2.1g
Protein	< 0.2 g
Cholesterol	< 0 mg
Sodium	246 mg

* Percent Daily Values are based on a 2,000 calorie diet.

Pasta from Athens

Ingredients

- 1 (16 oz.) package linguine pasta
- 1/2 C. chopped red onion
- 1 tbsp olive oil
- 2 cloves garlic, crushed
- 1 lb. skinless, boneless chicken breast meat - cut into bite-size pieces
- 1 (14 oz.) can marinated artichoke hearts, drained and chopped
- 1 large tomato, chopped
- 1/2 C. crumbled feta cheese
- 3 tbsps chopped fresh parsley
- 2 tbsps lemon juice
- 2 tsps dried oregano
- salt and pepper to taste
- 2 lemons, wedged, for garnish

Directions

- Cook your pasta in water and salt for 9 mins then remove all the liquids.
- Stir fry your garlic and onions in olive oil for 4 mins then add in the chicken and cook the mix until the chicken is fully done.
- Now set the heat to low and add the following: pasta, artichokes, oregano, tomato, lemon juice, feta, and parsley.
- Simmer this mix for 5 mins then shut the heat and add in pepper, salt, and lemon wedges.
- Enjoy.

Amount per serving (6 total)

Timing Information:

Preparation	15 m
Cooking	15 m
Total Time	30 m

Nutritional Information:

Calories	488 kcal
Fat	11.4 g
Carbohydrates	70g
Protein	32.6 g
Cholesterol	55 mg
Sodium	444 mg

* Percent Daily Values are based on a 2,000 calorie diet.

Greek Style Macaroni Salad

Ingredients

- 1/2 C. olive oil
- 1/2 C. red wine vinegar
- 1 1/2 tsps garlic powder
- 1 1/2 tsps dried basil
- 1 1/2 tsps dried oregano
- 3/4 tsp ground black pepper
- 3/4 tsp white sugar
- 2 1/2 C. cooked elbow macaroni
- 3 C. fresh sliced mushrooms
- 15 cherry tomatoes, halved
- 1 C. sliced red bell peppers
- 3/4 C. crumbled feta cheese
- 1/2 C. chopped green onions
- 1 (4 oz.) can whole black olives
- 3/4 C. sliced pepperoni sausage, cut into strips

Directions

- Get a bowl, combine: sugar, pepperoni, olive oil, olives, pasta, black pepper, onions, feta, mushrooms, red peppers, tomatoes, vinegar, oregano, garlic powder, and basil.
- Place a covering of plastic around the bowl and place everything in the fridge for 3 hrs.
- Enjoy.

Amount per serving (4 total)

Timing Information:

Preparation	15 m
Cooking	10 m
Total Time	2 h 25 m

Nutritional Information:

Calories	746 kcal
Fat	56.1 g
Carbohydrates	40.4g
Protein	22.1 g
Cholesterol	70 mg
Sodium	1279 mg

* Percent Daily Values are based on a 2,000 calorie diet.

Pita, Pesto, and Parmesan (Greek Style Bake)

Ingredients

- 1 (6 oz.) tub sun-dried tomato pesto
- 6 (6 inch) whole wheat pita breads
- 2 roma (plum) tomatoes, chopped
- 1 bunch spinach, rinsed and chopped
- 4 fresh mushrooms, sliced
- 1/2 C. crumbled feta cheese
- 2 tbsps grated Parmesan cheese
- 3 tbsps olive oil
- ground black pepper to taste

Directions

- Set your oven to 350 degrees before doing anything else.
- Coat each piece of pita with some pesto and then layer each with: pepper, tomatoes, olive oil, spinach, parmesan, mushrooms, and feta.
- Cook the bread, for 15 mins, in the oven, and then cut them into triangles before serving.
- Enjoy.

Amount per serving (6 total)

Timing Information:

Preparation	10 m
Cooking	12 m
Total Time	22 m

Nutritional Information:

Calories	350 kcal
Fat	17.1 g
Carbohydrates	41.6g
Protein	11.6 g
Cholesterol	13 mg
Sodium	587 mg

* Percent Daily Values are based on a 2,000 calorie diet.

Greek Spinach Puff Pastry Bake

Ingredients

- 3 tbsps olive oil
- 1 large onion, chopped
- 1 bunch green onions, chopped
- 2 cloves garlic, minced
- 2 lbs spinach, rinsed and chopped
- 1/2 C. chopped fresh parsley
- 2 eggs, lightly beaten
- 1/2 C. ricotta cheese
- 1 C. crumbled feta cheese
- 8 sheets phyllo dough
- 1/4 C. olive oil

Directions

- Coat a baking pan with nonstick spray and then set your oven to 350 degrees before doing anything else.
- Stir fry your garlic, onions, and green onions in olive oil for 4 mins. Then add in, the parsley and the spinach, and cook it all for 3 more mins.
- Remove all the contents.
- Get a bowl, combine: feta, onion mix, ricotta, and eggs.
- Coat a piece of phyllo with olive oil then layer it in the pan.
- Add another piece and also more olive oil.
- Do this two more times.
- Add your ricotta mix and fold the phyllo around the filling and seal it.
- Cook everything in the oven for 35 mins.

- Then cut the contents into your preferred shape.
- Enjoy.

Amount per serving (5 total)

Timing Information:

Preparation	30 m
Cooking	1 h
Total Time	1 h 30 m

Nutritional Information:

Calories	528 kcal
Fat	36.7 g
Carbohydrates	32.8g
Protein	21 g
Cholesterol	108 mg
Sodium	925 mg

* Percent Daily Values are based on a 2,000 calorie diet.

Greek Spinach Puff Pastry Bake

Ingredients

- 3 tbsps olive oil
- 1 large onion, chopped
- 1 bunch green onions, chopped
- 2 cloves garlic, minced
- 2 lbs spinach, rinsed and chopped
- 1/2 C. chopped fresh parsley
- 2 eggs, lightly beaten
- 1/2 C. ricotta cheese
- 1 C. crumbled feta cheese
- 8 sheets phyllo dough
- 1/4 C. olive oil

Directions

- Coat a baking pan with nonstick spray and then set your oven to 350 degrees before doing anything else.
- Stir fry your garlic, onions, and green onions in olive oil for 4 mins. Then add in, the parsley and the spinach, and cook it all for 3 more mins.
- Remove all the contents.
- Get a bowl, combine: feta, onion mix, ricotta, and eggs.
- Coat a piece of phyllo with olive oil then layer it in the pan.
- Add another piece and also more olive oil.
- Do this two more times.
- Add your ricotta mix and fold the phyllo around the filling and seal it.
- Cook everything in the oven for 35 mins.

- Then cut the contents into your preferred shape.
- Enjoy.

Amount per serving (5 total)

Timing Information:

Preparation	30 m
Cooking	1 h
Total Time	1 h 30 m

Nutritional Information:

Calories	528 kcal
Fat	36.7 g
Carbohydrates	32.8g
Protein	21 g
Cholesterol	108 mg
Sodium	925 mg

* Percent Daily Values are based on a 2,000 calorie diet.

Souvlaki III

Ingredients

Marinade:

- 3/4 C. balsamic vinaigrette salad dressing
- 3 tbsps lemon juice
- 1 tbsp dried oregano
- 1/2 tsp freshly ground black pepper
- 4 skinless, boneless chicken breast halves

White Sauce:

- 1/2 C. seeded, shredded cucumber
- 1 tsp kosher salt
- 1 C. plain yogurt
- 1/4 C. sour cream
- 1 tbsp lemon juice
- 1/2 tbsp rice vinegar
- 1 tsp olive oil
- 1 clove garlic, minced
- 1 tbsp chopped fresh dill
- 1/2 tsp Greek seasoning
- kosher salt to taste
- freshly ground black pepper to taste
- 4 large pita bread rounds
- 1 heart of romaine lettuce, cut into 1/4 inch slices
- 1 red onion, thinly sliced
- 1 tomato, halved and sliced
- 1/2 C. kalamata olives
- 1/2 C. pepperoncini
- 1 C. crumbled feta cheese

Directions

- Get a bowl, combine: chicken, black pepper (1/2 tsp), balsamic, oregano, and the juice of half of a lemon.
- Place a covering on the bowl and place the contents in the fridge for 2 hrs.
- Get a 2nd bowl and add in your cucumbers after shredding them and also some kosher salt.
- Let this stand for 10 mins.
- Get a 3rd bowl, combine: olive oil, garlic, yogurt, dill, rice vinegar, Greek seasoning, sour cream, and 1 tbsp of lemon juice.
- Place this mix in the fridge.
- Now grill your chicken pieces for 9 mins then flip them and cook the chicken pieces for 9 more mins.
- Let the chicken cool and then julienne it.
- Grill your pieces of pita for 3 mins and flip them throughout the entire grilling time.
- Fill each piece of pita with: pepperoncini, chicken, olive, lettuce, tomato, and onions.
- Add a topping of white sauce from the fridge and some feta on the side.
- Enjoy.

Amount per serving (4 total)

Timing Information:

Preparation	30 m
Cooking	20 m
Total Time	1 h 50 m

Nutritional Information:

Calories	764 kcal
Fat	40.5 g
Carbohydrates	55.9g
Protein	44.4 g
Cholesterol	133 mg
Sodium	3170 mg

* Percent Daily Values are based on a 2,000 calorie diet.

Easy Greek Style Chicken Breasts

Ingredients

- 2 tbsps all-purpose flour, divided
- 1/2 tsp salt
- 1/4 tsp black pepper
- 1/4 lb. feta cheese, crumbled
- 1 tbsp fresh lemon juice
- 1 tsp dried oregano
- 6 boneless, skinless chicken breast halves, flatten to 1/2 thickness
- 2 tbsps olive oil
- 1 1/2 C. water
- 1 cube chicken bouillon, crumbled
- 2 C. loosely packed torn fresh spinach leaves
- 1 ripe tomato, chopped

Directions

- Get a bowl, mix: oregano, cheese, and lemon juice.
- Get a 2nd bowl, combine: bouillon, 1 C. of water, and flour.
- Dredge you chicken in a mix of pepper, salt, and flour.
- Then fold each piece and stake a toothpick through each one.
- Sear the chicken in oil for 3 mins per side. Then top the chicken with the contents of the 2nd bowl.
- Cook everything for 1 more min before adding tomatoes and spinach.
- Get everything boiling and then place a lid on the pot.

- Set the heat to low and let it all cook for 12 mins.
- Enjoy.

Amount per serving (6 total)

Timing Information:

Preparation	20 m
Cooking	20 m
Total Time	40 m

Nutritional Information:

Calories	239 kcal
Fat	10.2 g
Carbohydrates	4.8g
Protein	31 g
Cholesterol	85 mg
Sodium	686 mg

* Percent Daily Values are based on a 2,000 calorie diet.

Baked Greek Potatoes

Ingredients

- 1/3 C. olive oil
- 1 1/2 C. water
- 2 cloves garlic, finely chopped
- 1/4 C. fresh lemon juice
- 1 tsp dried thyme
- 1 tsp dried rosemary
- 2 cubes chicken bouillon
- ground black pepper to taste
- 6 potatoes, peeled and quartered

Directions

- Set your oven to 350 degrees before doing anything else.
- Get a bowl, combine: pepper, olive oil, bouillon, water, rosemary, water, thyme, garlic, and lemon juice.
- Layer the potatoes in a casserole dish and top everything with the lemon mix.
- Place some foil around the dish and cook the contents in the oven for 90 mins.
- Flip the potatoes every 30 mins while cooking.
- Enjoy.

Amount per serving (4 total)

Timing Information:

Preparation	20 m
Cooking	2 h
Total Time	2 h 20 m

Nutritional Information:

Calories	418 kcal
Fat	18.5 g
Carbohydrates	58.6g
Protein	7 g
Cholesterol	< 1 mg
Sodium	< 596 mg

* Percent Daily Values are based on a 2,000 calorie diet.

Greek Rice

Ingredients

- 1/3 C. olive oil
- 2 onions, chopped
- 2 lbs fresh spinach, rinsed and stemmed
- 1 (8 oz.) can tomato sauce
- 2 C. water
- 1 tsp dried dill weed
- 1 tsp dried parsley
- salt and pepper to taste
- 1/2 C. uncooked white rice

Directions

- Stir fry your onions in olive oil until see-through then add in: spinach, water, and tomato sauce.
- Get everything boiling and then add: pepper, parsley, salt, and dill.
- Cook the mix for 2 mins while boiling then add the rice.
- Set the heat to low and cook everything for 27 mins.
- Enjoy.

Amount per serving (4 total)

Timing Information:

Preparation	5 m
Cooking	45 m
Total Time	50 m

Nutritional Information:

Calories	337 kcal
Fat	19.3 g
Carbohydrates	35.7g
Protein	9.8 g
Cholesterol	0 mg
Sodium	553 mg

* Percent Daily Values are based on a 2,000 calorie diet.

Parsley Pasta Salad

Ingredients

- 2 (9 oz.) packages cheese tortellini
- 1/2 C. extra virgin olive oil
- 1/4 C. lemon juice
- 1/4 C. red wine vinegar
- 2 tbsps chopped fresh parsley
- 1 tsp dried oregano
- 1/2 tsp salt
- 6 eggs
- 1 lb. baby spinach leaves
- 1 C. crumbled feta cheese
- 1/2 C. slivered red onion

Directions

- Boil your pasta in water and salt for 9 mins then remove all the liquids.
- Get a bowl, mix: salt, olive oil, oregano, lemon juice, pasta, parsley, and vinegar.
- Stir the contents and then place everything in the fridge for 3 hrs.
- Get your eggs boiling in water, place a lid on the pot, and shut the heat.
- Let the eggs stand for 15 mins. Then peel, and cut them into quarters.
- Take out the bowl in the fridge and add in: onions, eggs, feta, and spinach.
- Stir everything before serving.
- Enjoy.

Amount per serving (8 total)

Timing Information:

Preparation	15 m
Cooking	15 m
Total Time	2 h 30 m

Nutritional Information:

Calories	486 kcal
Fat	30.3 g
Carbohydrates	35.7g
Protein	19.8 g
Cholesterol	196 mg
Sodium	836 mg

* Percent Daily Values are based on a 2,000 calorie diet.

Orzo Salad II

Ingredients

- 1 C. uncooked orzo pasta
- 1/4 C. pitted green olives
- 1 C. diced feta cheese
- 3 tbsps chopped fresh parsley
- 3 tbsps chopped fresh dill
- 1 ripe tomato, chopped
- 1/4 C. virgin olive oil
- 1/8 C. lemon juice
- salt and pepper to taste

Directions

- Cook your orzo in boiling water with salt for 9 mins.
- Then remove the liquid and run the pasta under cool water.
- Now get a bowl, combine: tomato, olive, dill, feta, parsley, and orzo.
- Get a 2nd bowl, mix: lemon juice pepper, salt, and oil.
- Combine both bowls and toss everything.
- Place the mix in the fridge until cold.
- Enjoy.

Amount per serving (6 total)

Timing Information:

Preparation	15 m
Cooking	10 m
Total Time	25 m

Nutritional Information:

Calories	329 kcal
Fat	19.6 g
Carbohydrates	28.1g
Protein	10.9 g
Cholesterol	37 mg
Sodium	614 mg

* Percent Daily Values are based on a 2,000 calorie diet.

Mediterranean Dijon Shrimp Salad

Ingredients

Dijon Vinaigrette:

- 1/4 C. rice wine vinegar
- 2 tbsps Dijon mustard
- 1 large clove garlic, minced
- Big pinch of salt
- Black pepper, to taste
- 2/3 C. extra-virgin olive oil

Pasta Salad:

- 2 medium zucchini, thinly sliced lengthwise
- 1 medium yellow pepper, halved lengthwise, seeded
- 2 tbsps olive oil
- Ground black pepper and salt, to taste
- 1 gallon water
- 2 tbsps salt
- 1 lb. medium pasta shells
- 1 lb. cooked shrimp, halved lengthwise
- 8 oz. cherry tomatoes, halved
- 3/4 C. coarsely chopped, pitted Kalamata olives
- 1 C. crumbled feta cheese
- 1/2 small red onion, cut into small dice
- 2 tsps dried oregano

Directions

- Combine the following in a jar, then shake: pepper, wine vinegar, salt, mustard, and garlic.

Cooking with Olive Oil

- Coat your bell pepper and zucchini with olive oil (2 tbsps), pepper, and salt, then cook them under the broiler for 6 mins then flip them and broil for 5 more mins.
- Place them in a bowl after dicing them.
- Boil your pasta in water and salt for 9 mins then remove all the liquids.
- Now mix the pasta, veggies, and dressing together in a bowl and stir the mix.
- Enjoy.

Amount per serving (6 total)

Timing Information:

Preparation	35 m
Cooking	17 m
Total Time	1 h 22 m

Nutritional Information:

Calories	802 kcal
Fat	45.7 g
Carbohydrates	65.8g
Protein	33.6 g
Cholesterol	185 mg
Sodium	3398 mg

* Percent Daily Values are based on a 2,000 calorie diet.

Easy Greek Penne and Steak

Ingredients

- 8 oz. whole wheat penne pasta
- 2 tbsps extra virgin olive oil
- 1 tbsp butter
- 1 (1 lb.) beef rib eye steak
- 1 tbsp butter
- 1 tsp minced garlic
- 1/4 C. chopped shallots
- 1 tbsp soy sauce
- 1/2 C. sun-dried tomato pesto
- 1/2 C. sliced black olives
- 1 C. chopped fresh spinach
- 1 tsp basil
- 1 tbsp chopped parsley
- 1/2 C. crumbled feta cheese
- 3 tbsps sunflower kernels

Directions

- Boil your pasta in water and salt for 9 mins then remove all the liquids.
- Place the pasta in a bowl and coat the noodles with some olive oil.
- Brown your steak in some butter for 9 mins. Then cut the steak into pieces.
- Add in more butter and stir fry your shallots and garlic in it.
- Cook this for 2 mins then add the steak back in and cook the mix for 6 more mins.
- Add in the soy sauce and cook for 1 more min.
- Shut the heat and combine in: sunflower kernels, pesto, feta, olive, parsley, basil, and spinach.
- Add in the pasta to the pan and toss everything.

- Enjoy.

Amount per serving (4 total)

Timing Information:

Preparation	15 m
Cooking	20 m
Total Time	35 m

Nutritional Information:

Calories	579 kcal
Fat	35 g
Carbohydrates	44.7g
Protein	24.5 g
Cholesterol	73 mg
Sodium	710 mg

* Percent Daily Values are based on a 2,000 calorie diet.

Rustic Potatoes with Oregano and Olives

Ingredients

- 2 1/2 lbs potatoes, peeled and cubed
- 1/3 C. olive oil
- 2 cloves garlic, minced
- 3/4 C. whole, pitted kalamata olives
- 1 1/3 C. chopped tomatoes
- 1 tsp dried oregano
- salt and pepper to taste

Directions

- Stir fry your garlic, olives, and potatoes for 7 mins then add in the oregano and tomatoes.
- Place a lid on the pot and gently boil everything for 35 mins until the veggies are soft.
- Simmer the contents with a low heat and once the potatoes are done top everything with some pepper and salt.
- Enjoy.

Amount per serving (6 total)

Timing Information:

Preparation	25 m
Cooking	30 m
Total Time	55 m

Nutritional Information:

Calories	309 kcal
Fat	16.7 g
Carbohydrates	36.7g
Protein	4.5 g
Cholesterol	0 mg
Sodium	289 mg

* Percent Daily Values are based on a 2,000 calorie diet.

Cooking with Olive Oil

Shrimp with Feta and Tomatoes

Ingredients

- 4 tbsps extra virgin olive oil
- 1 medium onion, finely chopped
- 3/4 C. chopped green onion
- 2 cloves garlic, crushed
- 2 C. chopped, peeled tomatoes
- 1/2 C. dry white wine
- 1/4 C. chopped fresh parsley
- 1 tbsp chopped fresh oregano
- salt and pepper to taste
- 2 lbs large uncooked shrimp, peeled
- 4 oz. crumbled feta cheese

Directions

- Stir fry your onions until see through.
- Add in garlic and green onions.
- Cook for 4 more mins.
- Now add in: pepper, tomatoes, salt, wine and parsley.
- Place a cover on the pot and gently boil everything with a low level of heat for 35 mins.

- Now set your oven to 500 degrees before doing anything else.
- Layer half of the sauce into a casserole dish and top everything with the shrimp and add more sauce.
- Add a finally layering of feta over everything.
- Cook the contents in the oven for 13 mins then top with some more parsley.
- Enjoy.

Amount per serving (8 total)

Timing Information:

Preparation	30 m
Cooking	15 m
Total Time	45 m

Nutritional Information:

Calories	218 kcal
Fat	10.9 g
Carbohydrates	5.2g
Protein	21.4 g
Cholesterol	185 mg
Sodium	436 mg

* Percent Daily Values are based on a 2,000 calorie diet.

Classical Mediterranean Salad Dressing

Ingredients

- 2/3 C. olive oil
- 1/3 C. fresh lemon juice
- 1/3 C. tahini
- 1 tbsp nutritional yeast
- 1/4 C. tamari
- 1 tbsp honey
- 1/2 tsp dried oregano
- 1 tbsp mayonnaise
- salt and pepper to taste

Directions

- Process the following with a food processor until smooth: pepper, olive oil, salt, lemon juice, mayo, tahini, oregano, yeast, honey, and tamari.
- Place the contents in a jar or bowl with a seal or a covering of plastic and place everything in the fridge for 5 hrs.
- Enjoy.

Amount per serving (12 total)

Timing Information:

Preparation	
Cooking	5 m
Total Time	5 h 5 m

Nutritional Information:

Calories	167 kcal
Fat	16.5 g
Carbohydrates	4g
Protein	2.1 g
Cholesterol	< 1 mg
Sodium	< 347 mg

* Percent Daily Values are based on a 2,000 calorie diet.

Mediterrean Asian Salad Dressing

Ingredients

- 1/2 C. tahini (sesame paste)
- 1/2 C. olive oil
- 1/2 C. water
- 1/4 C. tamari (dark soy sauce)
- 2 tbsps red wine vinegar
- 2 tbsps lemon juice
- 2 tsps minced fresh ginger root
- 2 cloves garlic, pressed
- black pepper to taste

Directions

- Process the following in a food processor for 2 mins: pepper, tahini, garlic, olive oil, ginger, water, lemon juice, tamari, and vinegar.
- Place the contents in a jar or bowl with a lid or covering of plastic and place everything in the fridge for 5 hrs.
- Enjoy.

Amount per serving (16 total)

Timing Information:

Preparation	
Cooking	10 m
Total Time	5 h 10 m

Nutritional Information:

Calories	109 kcal
Fat	10.8 g
Carbohydrates	2.3g
Protein	< 1.8 g
Cholesterol	0 mg
Sodium	258 mg

* Percent Daily Values are based on a 2,000 calorie diet.

Homemade Balsamic Salad Dressing

Ingredients

- 3 tbsps extra virgin olive oil
- 2 tbsps balsamic vinegar
- 1/2 tsp dried oregano
- salt and pepper to taste

Directions

- Combine the following in a small bowl: pepper, olive oil, oregano, and balsamic.
- Enjoy at room temp.

Amount per serving (3 total)

Timing Information:

Preparation	
Cooking	5 m
Total Time	5 m

Nutritional Information:

Calories	129 kcal
Fat	13.5 g
Carbohydrates	1.7g
Protein	< 0.1 g
Cholesterol	< 0 mg
Sodium	196 mg

* Percent Daily Values are based on a 2,000 calorie diet.

Sesame Blueberry Salad Dressing

Ingredients

- 1/2 C. olive oil
- 1/2 C. white vinegar
- 1/4 C. fresh blueberries
- 1 lemon, juiced
- 1 tsp sesame seeds

Directions

- For 2 mins, with a blender, pulse the following with a low speed: lemon juice, olive oil, and blue berries.
- Pour the contents into a mason jar and then add in your sesame seeds.
- Shake everything and serve at room temp or chilled.
- Enjoy.

Amount per serving (10 total)

Timing Information:

Preparation	
Cooking	10 m
Total Time	10 m

Nutritional Information:

Calories	101 kcal
Fat	11 g
Carbohydrates	1g
Protein	< 0.1 g
Cholesterol	< 0 mg
Sodium	< 1 mg

* Percent Daily Values are based on a 2,000 calorie diet.

Latin Omelet

Ingredients

- 1/2 C. olive oil
- 1/2 lb potatoes, thinly sliced
- salt and pepper to taste
- 1 large onion, thinly sliced
- 4 eggs
- salt and pepper to taste
- 2 tomatoes - peeled, seeded, and coarsely diced
- 2 green onions, diced

Directions

- Coat your potatoes with pepper and salt then fry them in olive oil until golden.
- Now add in the onions and cook the mix for 7 mins until the onions are soft.
- At the same time whisk your eggs with some pepper and salt then add the mix to the potatoes and onions.
- Set the heat to low and continue cooking everything until the eggs become brown at the bottom.
- Push a fork under the omelet to slightly loosen it then place a plate on top of the pan.
- Now flip the pan. Then place the flipped omelet back in the pan.
- Cook the omelet on its opposite side until the eggs become somewhat crispy.
- Top everything with some green onions and tomatoes.
- Enjoy.

Amount per serving (6 total)

Timing Information:

Preparation	15 m
Cooking	45 m
Total Time	1 h

Nutritional Information:

Calories	252 kcal
Fat	21.5 g
Carbohydrates	10.7g
Protein	5.4 g
Cholesterol	124 mg
Sodium	54 mg

* Percent Daily Values are based on a 2,000 calorie diet.

Coconut Chicken Breast

Ingredients

- 1 tsp ground cumin
- 1 tsp ground cayenne pepper
- 1 tsp ground turmeric
- 1 tsp ground coriander
- 4 skinless, boneless chicken breast halves
- salt and pepper to taste
- 2 tbsps olive oil
- 1 onion, diced
- 1 tbsp minced fresh ginger
- 2 jalapeno peppers, seeded and diced
- 2 cloves garlic, minced
- 3 tomatoes, seeded and diced
- 1 (14 oz.) can light coconut milk
- 1 bunch diced fresh parsley

Directions

- Get a bowl, combine: coriander, cumin, turmeric, and cayenne.
- Add in the chicken and some pepper and salt.
- Stir the contents to evenly coat the chicken with the spices.
- Now for 12 mins per side fry your chicken in 1 tbsp of olive oil until fully done then place it to the side.
- Add the rest of the olive oil to the pan and begin to stir fry the garlic, onions, jalapenos, and ginger for 7 mins.
- Now add in the tomatoes and cook the mix for 7 more mins before adding the coconut milk.
- Top the chicken with the tomato mix and some parsley then serve.

- Enjoy.

Amount per serving (4 total)

Timing Information:

Preparation	15 m
Cooking	30 m
Total Time	45 m

Nutritional Information:

Calories	345 kcal
Fat	19.9 g
Carbohydrates	11.5g
Protein	29.3 g
Cholesterol	72 mg
Sodium	234 mg

* Percent Daily Values are based on a 2,000 calorie diet.

Ensalada Roja con Pollo
(Latin Potato Salad)

Ingredients

- 6 large baking potatoes, peeled and cubed
- 4 carrots, diced
- 1 tbsp olive oil
- 1 large onion, diced
- 3 C. diced cooked chicken
- 6 hard-cooked eggs, peeled and diced
- 2 dill pickles, diced
- 2 tbsps dill pickle brine
- 2 C. mayonnaise
- salt and pepper to taste
- 1 C. diced cooked beets

Directions

- Submerge your carrots and potatoes in a big pot, in water, and get everything boiling.
- Continue boiling the contents until the potatoes are soft for 12 mins then remove all the liquids.
- Now begin to stir fry your onions in olive oil for 12 mins then remove them from the pan.
- Get a bowl, combine: pickles, potatoes, eggs, carrots, and chicken.
- Get a 2nd bowl, combine: mayo, onion, and pickle juice.

- Now combine both bowls and add some pepper and salt.
- Place the contents in the fridge with a covering of plastic for 2 hrs.
- Enjoy.

Amount per serving (12 total)

Timing Information:

Preparation	25 m
Cooking	15 m
Total Time	2 h 40 m

Nutritional Information:

Calories	540 kcal
Fat	35.8 g
Carbohydrates	38.7g
Protein	17.4 g
Cholesterol	146 mg
Sodium	475 mg

* Percent Daily Values are based on a 2,000 calorie diet.

Broccoli Bake I

(Red Onions and Sage)

Ingredients

- 1 (12 oz.) bag broccoli florets
- 1/2 red onion, sliced
- 8 fresh sage leaves, torn
- 2 tbsps extra-virgin olive oil
- 1/2 tsp salt
- 1/2 tsp garlic salt
- 1/4 tsp ground black pepper

Directions

- Cover a casserole dish or sheet for baking with foil and then set your oven to 400 degrees before doing anything else.
- Layer your broccoli evenly throughout the dish and top with sage leaves and onions. Garnish all the veggies with olive oil and then black pepper, regular salt, and garlic salt.
- Cook the veggies in the oven for 27 mins until slightly browned and crunchy.
- Enjoy.

Amount per serving (4 total)

Timing Information:

Preparation	Cooking	Total Time
10 m	20 m	30 m

Nutritional Information:

Calories	97 kcal
Fat	7.1 g
Carbohydrates	7.3g
Protein	2.6 g
Cholesterol	0 mg
Sodium	546 mg

* Percent Daily Values are based on a 2,000 calorie diet.

Italian Style Broccoli and Pasta

Ingredients

- 1 lb spicy Italian sausage
- 1/2 C. olive oil
- 4 cloves garlic, minced
- 1 (16 oz.) package cavatelli pasta
- 1 (16 oz.) package frozen broccoli
- 1/2 tsp crushed red pepper flakes
- 1/4 C. grated Parmesan cheese

Directions

- Boil your pasta in salt and water for 10 mins. At the 7 min mark add in your broccoli to the boiling pasta. Then remove all the liquid after 10 mins of total boiling time.
- Simultaneously stir fry your sausage and set it aside after removing all the drippings.
- Add in the olive oil and the garlic and cook until golden in color.
- Get a big bowl, toss: broccoli, sausage, cavatelli, garlic, and olive oil.
- Top the mix with parmesan and pepper flakes.
- Enjoy.

Amount per serving (8 total)

Timing Information:

Preparation	Cooking	Total Time
5 m	30 m	35 m

Nutritional Information:

Calories	548 kcal
Fat	33 g
Carbohydrates	45.5g
Protein	18.4 g
Cholesterol	45 mg
Sodium	470 mg

* Percent Daily Values are based on a 2,000 calorie diet.

EASY BROCCOLI STIR FRY

Ingredients

- 1 lb broccoli florets
- 3 tbsps finely grated Parmesan cheese
- 1 tsp brown sugar
- 2 tbsps olive oil
- 1 tsp red pepper flakes
- 1/4 tsp kosher salt
- 1/8 tsp freshly ground black pepper

Directions

- Blanch your broccoli in boiling water for 60 seconds then immediately enter the veggies into some ice water.
- Now lay the broccoli on some paper towel to drain it completely.
- Get a bowl, combine: brown sugar and parmesan.
- Now get your oil hot then begin to stir fry the broccoli for a few secs then add in the black pepper, salt, and pepper flakes.
- Stir the broccoli then let everything cook for 3 mins.
- Shut the heat and top the veggie with the parmesan mix.
- Enjoy.

Amount per serving (4 total)

Timing Information:

Preparation	Cooking	Total Time
15 m	10 m	25 m

Nutritional Information:

Calories	81 kcal
Fat	5.6 g
Carbohydrates	6.2g
Protein	3.2 g
Cholesterol	2 mg
Sodium	< 144 mg

* Percent Daily Values are based on a 2,000 calorie diet.

THANKS FOR READING! JOIN THE CLUB AND KEEP ON COOKING WITH 6 MORE COOKBOOKS....

http://bit.ly/1TdrStv

Cooking with Olive Oil

To grab the box sets simply follow the link mentioned above, or tap one of book covers.

This will take you to a page where you can simply enter your email address and a PDF version of the box sets will be emailed to you.

Hope you are ready for some serious cooking!

http://bit.ly/1TdrStv

Cooking with Olive Oil

Come On...
Let's Be Friends :)

We adore our readers and love connecting with them socially.

Like BookSumo on Facebook and let's get social!

Facebook

And also check out the BookSumo Cooking Blog.

Food Lover Blog

24229861R00095

Printed in Great Britain
by Amazon